For all the girls and women
we have ever been

First published in the UK in 2020 by Stour Valley Publishing

A CIP Catalogue Record of this book is available from the British Library

ISBN: 978-1-913450-30-4 (PB)

Printed & Bound by Mixam UK Ltd, Watford, UK for:

Stour Valley Publishing
N4 Blois Meadow Business Centre
Blois Road, Steeple Bumpstead
Haverhill
Suffolk
CB9 7BN
www.stourvalleypublishing.co.uk

For Bibby.

Cover photo credit:
@augustinewong, with thanks for this and other imagery in this collection to unsplash.com.

Original imagery of Henny by Helena g Anderson.

"This spoke right to my heart."

"I read this as my mother's voice speaking to me. And now quietly sniffling in the loo at the office. But in a good open hearted way."

"I can't tell you how much this has moved me."

"Love your 'My darling girls'... yes book please!!
I need to give one to my
daughter! And keep one for me!!"

"I just love your posts - your words are so inspirational, uplifting and motivating - yet also very moving and emotional. I want to keep reading them and share them with my girls too."

"Each letter is poignant, honest and relatable."

"This is a keeper - for all those times when we question ourselves, our whole being, our worthiness, our validity, our space on this planet! It's a keeper, so eloquently read in a few words."

"Yesterday I was clever,
so I wanted to change the world.
Today I am wise, so I am
changing myself."
Rumi

My darling girl

These words arrived on the pages of my journal just when I needed them most.

I was never quite sure where they came from, or how to describe them, other than a form of love letter... or simply, poetry-ish. What I do know is their messages helped me navigate the long journey to here.

I offer them up in case they bring something useful for you too.

The invitation is to dip in, perhaps to hold a thought in your heart and pick a page. Or maybe you'll choose to begin at the end? It can be a lovely place to start.

With love

Henny

My darling girl

It is you I have been writing to.
You who has been hiding in my wings.
Not sure if you were loveable enough.
Come out into the light, sweet one.
You are worthy of all my love.
You are worthy of the sunlight on your skin,
The breeze in your hair,
The birdsong in your ears,
The taste of all that is sweet and true in your
mouth.
You are worthy of all that there is.
You are whole.
And you are loved.
Hide no more within this cloak you made,
So well fashioned it had become a second skin.
Let us unfasten its clasp.
Let us drop it to the ground.
Let us thank it for its years of service.
And step free.

My darling girl

In these times, when change feels like a
toddler's game
When it's hard to know which way to play
Remember
Take time for what it is you need
Open your heart when you need to grieve
Open your belly when you need to breathe
Open your mind when you need to see
Open your soul when you need to heal
Open your ears when you need to be heard
Open your hand when you need to be held
My darling child
In these times
Remember
Cry your tears
Feel your pain
Hold each other close again
Share your hopes
Soothe your fears
And last, my dear, remember
Love is what outlasts the years.

My darling girl

Show me what makes your tears fall
Show me what makes you tremble before dawn
breaks
Show me what makes your heart sing
Show me everything that brought you to this
place
Show me your tiny joys
Your woes
Your ancient fears
Show me all of who you are
And I will show you love
I will show you how broad is the sweep of my
arms,
As I hold you tight
I will show you the expansiveness of my ever opening
heart,
That has space for every part of you
I will show you there are no scales upon which
to be weighed
There are no measures that can find you
wanting
I will show you there are no conditions for my
love of you
I will show you there is just my love and you
Which added up makes one, not two

My darling girl

Change is not linear.
It ebbs and flows with the waters of the estuary.
The rising tide carrying you in her arms,
Rushing into an inlet and returning you back as
fast, from whence you came
At times
She strands you on the sands;
High and dry I see your fear you may never feel
her rush and tug once more
Or you despair the wildness of her pull - swept off
your feet into channels unforeseen
At times
The water's rise is too subtle for your eye.
You wait impatient for land to fall away from
beneath your feet.
But your ancient heart feels the timeless current
and knows that all is flow
And so, fall in again with the streaming tide
Gather experience as shingle from beaches you
pass by... and release them, to be pulled back out to
sea, and gather more again
Each time
You bring new treasure scattered with precious
pearls of wisdom that do not slip your hold
And so your progress ebbs and flows
And you change
Learning
The only constant is the constancy of life's tide
drawing you ever
Inward
Outward
Onward

My darling girl

Bring the calming hand of love
To your own heart
And settle her with a kiss
Know this
You are your own beloved
You are your own parent / child
You are the wild spirit and the untethered soul
And
You hold the source of succour
Within your palms
Turn your love toward yourself
And rest there
Now place one hand in mine
And fly through the mountains of your mind
Journeying home
To here
And hear
Your heart's desire

My darling girl

Fear bows your head
Fear makes you avoid the stranger's eye
(Fearing it is the eye of the storm)
Fear holds you tight
Fear holds you small
Fear bares its teeth,
(Fearing it will be bitten first)
Fear is afraid
Fear is seeking solace
Fear is asking to be held
Fear is a small child in the dark
So
Look up
Greet the stranger and the friend alike
Turn on the light of your smile
And remember
Fear may bark
But it cannot bite.

My darling girl

You ask me what it is to remember.

You ask me if it is an imprint of past lives, past experiences, past people, past places, past loves, past loss, past pain, past hope, past opportunity, past benediction, past abandonment, past finding ourselves. You ask if that is what you feel when you remember.

I say yes, if that is what helps you. You ask what else it can be. I say...

It can be a sensation of falling into water and never drown. A sensation of being held in air, where you can never fall. A sensation of walking through flames that can never burn. A sensation of the wind in your hair but not one strand moves.

The act of remembering is an act of standing perfectly still inside yourself, present and connected. Not reaching out to a memory, simply ready to receive.

The act of remembering is one of surrender, my love. It is being willing to understand without judgement or shame. It is looking above and beneath and around. An act of curiosity about yourself and the space you inhabit. An act of listening within.

Acutely attuned to every nuance.

And yet.

The act of remembering is an act of forgetting all you have ever learnt. It is being an open vessel. No longer primed with the past, or watching the future. The act of remembering is one of accepting what is.

Entirely here. Entirely now.

That is all it is.

I see you smiling.

Do you remember now, my love?

My darling girl

There's an unsettle that comes
before we nestle.
Like the dog who circles their bed before
tucking themselves in beneath their tail
to sleep.
Like the bird that joins the wild symmetry of
the murmuration before roosting in the tree.
Like the child that has one last run around the
home before sleepy story time.
The unsettle is part of the process into finding
our space to rest.
It's a moment when our energies rise in order
that they can fall.
It's a time to see what is emerging, knowing it
will run its own sweet course.
We do not need to lean into it.
We do not need to control it.
We do not need to press against it and resist
what lies behind it.
We can simply be with it.
And see what it will be.

My darling girl

These fears that flutter around your heart are
just the little parts of you, trying to be heard.
Each tiny terror crafted from feathery what ifs;
imaginings of there and then combined.
They seek a place to land, to rest their weary
wings - a chance to roost so you can hear the
song each brings.
Your resistance to their settling is what gives
them flight. The love they hide within their fear
is what holds them tight.
Let them land, my love.
Hold out your hand, my love.
And, my love, dry the tears their frantic flight
excite.
Watch each descend onto your palm and listen
to their song. Stroke away the darkness slicked
on their wings and see the iridescent shine
beneath.
Name them without shaming them and count
them as you count your blessings. Each fear is
there to teach and while they fly you cannot
learn.
Give them a safe place to nest and they will rest,
and, when they have been heard, tuck their
head beneath their wings to sleep.

My darling girl

Come into the place where
the Quiet One speaks.
Hold her hand in comfort and be at peace.
In time she'll guide you to the water's edge
See there your self in its mirrored sheen.
See how you truly are.
Know this is where you've always been.
A breath can take you far.

My darling girl

Be kind, little one.
Remember.
To love your self fiercely.
To hold your self tenderly.
To listen to your self deeply.
To forgive your self swiftly.
Remember.
The drum of your heart beats the song of your
soul - and it sings of the glories of you.
Remember
What it is to be, little one.

My darling girl

Breaking rules is not for the faint of heart.
You have to know them well to understand their art.
And the rules you made yourself?
They can be the hardest ones to break.
Laying down your strictures, writing your own commandments and then always abiding by your word... oh, my love, do you not see how important it is to flex in order to then grow?
The secret is
Remember that which you create
you can unmake.
And remake.
And unmake.
And remake endlessly.
Because each age you reach has its own requirements and its own flow.
Understand what will serve you best before laying down your lore.

My darling girl

Here it comes again, that state of flux.
Just when you thought everything settled, die
cast, ink set, final thread woven through the
tapestry. And then.
A pin prick of awareness.
A sensation rumbling in the deepest distance.
At first ignorable.
'Oh that? I'm sure it's nothing, just carry on as
we are.'
Then more insistent.
'Look. It's fine, nothing to hear here.'
Then more insistent still.
'No, honestly. Just don't look at it and I'm sure
it'll go away.'
Until. Eventually.
'Hang on! This thing? Oh, I'm meant to notice
that? This rolling, frothing, churning, rumbling
thing that skitters all around, that all
consuming flood of awareness?'
Yes.
That.
That thing that takes more energy to ignore
than it could ever take to deal with.
That thing that makes so much noise you
believe it's bigger than you could ever be.
Yes.
That.
It's time to listen up, settle in.
And. Go. With. The. Flow.

My darling girl

We are as Russian dolls.
Layer upon layer of painted carapace shielding
our beating hearts.
With each release we reveal our self
more fully.
But.
Go gently in these tender times of change; each
skin you shed leaves you a little raw.
It's ok to take time to stretch and learn, to feel
how this fresh layer fits... until you're ready to
go a little deeper. And once more you brave the
prising apart of your prism, revealing the
glinting truth beneath.
For at your core are tiny dancing motes of light,
energetic crystal shards of the stars that we all
once were.

My darling girl

Take my hand.
And come with me,
Back to yourself.
Listen to your voice within
Be kind
Allow your breath to open up the spaces
between your ribs
Breathe out from the soles of your feet
And into the tips of your toes
Rebalance
Run
And rest
If your smile can't yet reach your face, grow it
deep inside your belly.
Let it linger there.
Slowly expanding with each breath,
warming you.
Feel it rise up your spine
and settle across your shoulders.
Draped in its mantle; rest in it. Don't wrestle
with it. There is no win, no lose. There just is.
Come back to yourself my love.
And be free.

My darling girl

Unbind your mind.
Unwrap the bandages that swaddle your
thoughts.
Lay out your limbs and allow air to flow freely
through your fingers and toes.
Stretch.
And stretch again.
Breathe.
Deeply into every cell.
Expanding with the lightness only air can bring.
Shine light into the darkest corners of your
thinking and shake off the dust sheets to let
every hidden desire gleam in the sunlight of
your love.
Let all stand free and wander amongst the
be-longings you have secreted there.
Unobstructed, deconstructed, unrestricted, your
thoughts will find a way to grow into what you
truly need.
So breathe.
Be freed.

My darling girl

**Yay!
Every day.**

My darling girl

You haven't spoken for a while.
I haven't heard your voice, felt you tug on my
sleeve, slip your hand into mine or whisper that
you need a hug.
I haven't found you sleeping in my bed, blanket
pulled up to your neck, knees tucked tight, face
in fierce concentration even in repose.
I haven't laid my hand upon your forehead,
checking you're ok.
I haven't tucked you in with a goodnight kiss
and Brahms lullaby.
I haven't.
I haven't.
And yet.
Here I've been.
With each sleep I've stood by. With each new
step I've been at your side. With each sigh I've
seen the smile that's not been long behind.
I've watched as you worked at quieting your
chattering mind. I've rested alongside you as
you calmed your beating heart. I've breathed
with you, deep into your belly and out,
throughout your limbs. And I've sat beside you
as you became still.
All this you have done, my love.
All this you have done on your own.
All this you have done, not alone.

My darling girl

I saw you move today.
I saw you run into the sun.
I saw you dance without a backward glance at
who was following your lead.
I saw you step toward the mountain top with a
jump skip hop.
I saw you breathe to relieve today tomorrow
and yesterday.
I saw you smile.
And it made my heart sing.

My darling girl

It's ok having nothing to say.
I see you struggling to form the words.
To shape the sounds that you think others
might want to hear.
To ease the meaning out of your heart and into
another's.
I see you face the blank paper.
Pencil sharpened, pen inked, desk tidied, ready
for the flow and tumble of consonants and
vowels, dripping with punctuation points.
I see you dig around in your mind, discarding
this that and the other as not worthy of your
penmanship - not worthy of your readership.
I see you ache in a desire to speak your truth
but find your truth has no words today.
And that's ok.
Sit still in the silent space.
Hold your truth within.
When it's ready, the words will begin.

My darling girl

Between discipline and surrender is flow.
Feel its waves washing through your body as you sit
here now. Start with your fingertips. Sense the tingle
as it drifts over the ridges of your knuckles. Feel it
softly pooling in your palms before drifting into
your wrists, rising to tingle in the subtlety of your
inner elbow. A feather light touch. Then up and
along the gentle curve of your arms into the inverted
gully of your shoulders. The tickle of a springtime
stream slipping down through your chest, skipping
over and around and through your softly beating
heart, your kidneys, liver, lungs. Feel it flow through
your inhale. Feel it flow through your exhale. Feel it
tumbling into your belly. And feel it rising up from
your shoulders too. Along your clavicle to the hollow
of your throat, swirling round your neck and up over
your chin. Cleansing your mouth your nose your
eyes your ears your mind your crown and down
across your tender face, the back of your head.
Bathing your whole self in its cool waters. All your
skin. Sensory. Alive. From your belly to your root
your hips your thighs knees ankles soles toes.
Teasing your toes. Softly dousing over and through
and around your whole body. Here. Now. Present.
Alert. Alive. Safe. Happy. Connected. Comfortable.
Knowledgeable. In tune. Feel the flow. It moves to
your rhythm. It is always there, in that liminal space,
between the discipline of doing, not doing and the
surrender of knowing, not knowing. Entirely yours.
Entirely for you. Allow yourself to feel it. Sit with it.
Sense it. Enjoy it. Go with it. Embrace it. Treasure it.
And release it.

My darling girl

No one has all the answers.
No one can tell you how it is, what to do, who to be. No one, however sound their intent, has the right to direct the way you live your life.
No one holds your plans in their hands and marks your choices with a fat red pen.
No one is your judge or jury.
No one owns the space where your act of choice resides.
I think you know this, my love.
At times of turbulence and doubt, I see you seeking. Looking for a teacher, guru, friend.
Someone to show the way.
I see your relief when one appears and holds out their answers with open arms, welcoming your sink into their embrace; releasing yourself from this burden of choice.
Turning your path to run alongside theirs.
It's a comforting anchor.
For a while.
I think you know this, my love.
I think you know the only one who can find your answers sits inside this mortal body that you wear.
I think you know you are your own teacher, guru, friend.
I think you know others are there to help light your way, to expand your range of choice - not limit it to choices they have made.
I think you know this, my love. And I think, as you need it, you will find you know it all.

My darling girl

Tell me where it hurts. Tell me what causes that
tension in your jaw. Tell me what stiffens your
shoulders and shortens your words.
Tell me of that secret ache, heart break, long
since mistake.
Tell me.
And in your telling, allow it.
And in your telling, free it.
And in your telling unbind, unwind, be kind to
yourself.
Hold yourself in endless care and cease this
striving to be strong.
I say this not to save you. For you do not need
saving. I say this because I see you are so closely
bound, nothing else can enter.
I say this because, dear heart, it is the cracks
within the seams that let the light come pouring
in.
Tender is the light, my love.
Let its dance begin.

My darling girl

I cannot see all the roads that you will travel.
Nor the ones you will travel with.
I cannot see the places you will visit, nor the
adventures you will live.
I cannot see the challenges you'll face up to, or
the love you've yet to give.
I cannot shield you from the rain clouds, nor
cloak you from the storm.
I cannot wrap you when the cold bites or shade
you when it's warm.
I cannot take every pebble from your pathway,
or tell you right from wrong.
I cannot choose your dancing partners, say
where you must reside.
These are all your choices, things just you must
decide.
I can only love you and stay here by your side.
And tell you, with my hand in yours,
I'm in it for the ride.

My darling girl

This is not a crisis.
This is an awakening. An emergence.
A resurgence of everything you have ever been,
all that you are and all you ever will be.
This is not mid-life, late-life, much-too-young-
to-know-anything-life. This is just life. Sticky,
messy, complicated, glorious, belly-laugh-filled,
spectacular, all-dancing all-singing, outlandish,
would-you-believe-it, tearful, quiet, lonely,
scared, is-this-all-there-is, can't-get-enough-of-
it. LIFE. A switchback ride, eternal tide of heart-
breaking, heart-making life.
Effervescent, ever present, incessant.
There's no judgement here. We are all learners
at this game. Everyone the same, whether lost
in love or pain.
And we can all be found.
So. Here you are. Safe and sound. Feet firmly on
the ground - entirely free to see the whole of
life, in its entirety

My darling girl

This moment. The exquisiteness of this moment. I see the hairs on your arms tremble in the flush and rush of the realisation that this is a moment.

Fleeting, transitory, a will-o-the-wisp of emotion that courses, flooding your veins, rising up through your body and erupting in the most glorious smile.

Dear heart, oh how I love it when I see you smile.

Your smile holds this moment. It cements it, marks it, puts a flag in the earth from which it sprang and declares this is your moment.

Hold it close, my love.

Through the years, the tears, the fears, let this smile shine bright within.

Nurture it, feed it, tend it. Water it. Give it the nourishment of time with friends, of self-care and deep compassion, of joy and love and dancing.

Give it the transportation of music, the exhilaration of the mountains, the cleansing beauty of the sea. Give it breath, give it your beating heart, give it the love you feel from me.

From your trembling belly, to your tingling toes, to the centre of your crown, feel the energy of this moment. And live it.

That is all, my love.

My darling girl

What a difference a day makes. That indelible
mark of yesterday's commotion of emotion -
softly, with the sun's rise, fades clear.
Fear, shame, anger, doubt, anxiety - these all
shall pass. Yet even as you feel their fleeting
touch so keenly and ache for their sisters - joy,
hope, faith, clarity, compassion - see they are
each there to teach. Do you see, my love? Their
mountains and valleys that line your path, they
are all essential to your journey.
Learning to accept their highs and lows, that is
the lesson.
Learning to remember this too shall pass, that is
the lesson.
Learning to love the lessons that they teach us,
that is the lesson.
As I watch you flow through this vast expanse of
knowledge, discovering what you have
somehow always known, I see your endless
cycle of learning, unlearning and relearning.
At times I stand with you, bathed in light on the
mountainside - at others I walk beside you
through the shadow of the valley. Wherever you
are on your journey know you are not alone.
Know that the sun always rises. Know that you
choose the path that will take you to what you
most need to know, in the time you need it
most. Ahh, my love, that may be the most
beautiful lesson of all.

My darling girl

You have the freedom to think.
And feel and believe and value and do what you will. You have the intuition.
The courage the skills the resources the resilience the power the strength the serenity to be who you will.
You have the heart. The hope the vision the creativity the spirit the joy the energy the flow to go where you will.
Each of these is a golden thread that you have spun across the years.
Take hold of all these threads my love and weave them with me. Capture each one and watch the fabric grow and shape into a cloak that wraps around your shoulders.
Wear it throughout the year that comes. Know that I have lined it with compassion, and fastened it with an unbreakable bond of self love. It suits you, this cloak.
You wear it well.

My darling girl

It's all still there. Those dreams you imagined
yesterday and felt crystallise with the dawn, they
held their shape with the rise and set of the sun.
Worry not that this day they seem hard to reach -
like in the night some unseen hand placed them
on a shelf too high to see.
Learning faith. It's hard when hope and optimism
evade us as fast as they arrive.
But this is part of the journey.
Learning to surrender to the highs and lows.
Do you see, my love? The mountains and valleys
that line your path - it's when you look back you
can see the full glory of their beauty.
This realisation is an endless loop of realisation
that realisation is an endless loop.
Like every piece of deep knowledge is gleaned
from multiple visits to a vast library where we've
endlessly reached for the same book, forgetting the
words that lie within, reading the same chapter,
paragraph, sentence. And as we read it, we say
'This! Yes! This I need to know!' And even as we
feel that spark of recognition it's as though we've
learnt it for the first time. Until it embeds. And we
move on to repeat the cycle of learning,
unlearning, relearning. Tomorrow you will see you
are a little taller and the day after, taller still. That
shelf where your dreams are tucked will become
within reach. And remember my darling the shelf
is of your making - and no one governs your
actions. Perhaps you can take the books of your
knowledge and, like a child, make a step on which
to climb?

My darling girl

Sometimes we cross the river of doubt with
ease, skipping across the stepping stones,
landing softly on the other side.
And sometimes we stare at the raging waters,
wondering how we ever thought we could
traverse them.
This doubt that flows through your mind is ever
present in each of us.
We all have it.
It's how we treat it that makes the difference.
Stepping into its cool waters, feeling the tug of
whatever wants to sweep us away and facing it
with gentle resistance, noticing it,
acknowledging it, exploring it - all this helps us
tame its turbulence. When we get braver we
swim through it, experiencing the eddies and
swirls that greet our limbs, as we sweep them
into its currents.
We sense our strength.
It can become a joyful thing, this exploration of
what tries to restrain us.
Then, as we reach the other side, we step up
onto land, and notice we are already dry.
We see that what we have swum through is an
old river bed.
The water was all of our own making.

My darling girl

Think of all the happy times. Think of frost
sparkling in the trees. Think of leaves softening
your step. Think of sand beneath your toes.
Think of sun on your skin. Think of cold biting
at your cheeks. Think of sweetly scented rooms.
Think of hands held in yours. Think of hugs
that warm your soul. Think of kisses light as air.
Think of friendships. Love. And care. Think of
who you've been with, and where. Think of
every happy moment, minute, hour, day,
month, year. Think of this life and all the times
there have been when your heart has sung and
your cheeks have ached with smiling.
Think of the constants there have been.
The threads that flow through all these times.
And remember that in truth there is just one.
One constant.
One thread.
One person who has always been in the centre
of this happiness.
You, of course, my love. It's you.

My darling girl

I see you sitting there. Putting on your brave face.
Holding up your head. Telling the world that
everything is good. Everything is fine. Everything
flows, aligned.

I see the tender wounds that have yet to heal, the way
you hold yourself close, shielding your heart from
prying eyes. I see the hurt within. I see. I see. I see.
And I understand that there is no salve I can apply.
No lotion or potion to ease this subtle ache. And I
understand that all I can do, my love, is hold you in
my arms and allow the tears to fall upon my shoulder,
to stroke your brow and smooth your hair and tell
how much I love you. How much I will always love
you, come pain or time. No matter where you are or
how your hurt makes you want to push against me. I
will always see you exactly as you are. Beautiful, bold
and wondrous.

Understand that this too shall pass. But while it is only
transitory, it offers up a gift. Experience it. Examine it.
Understand it. Seek all its facets and learn what you
can about it. About why it has the power to hurt.
And love it.

For in this moment you are alive. Awakened to your
senses.

We learn from all these sorrows. And that is the
hardest lesson.

Learn all you can. Seek an understanding of yourself
and your situation and pluck those two arrows from
your breast.

Then remember my darling, that while we cannot
always avoid the first arrow, with the second we have a
choice. The second is our response to the first.
And it is of our own making.

My darling girl

You have been talking of surrender.
Of shedding your tears and fears. Of dispelling
half truths of how and who you are.
You tell me this place of surrender shines in the
distance, but that the path is hard. You speak of
stones beneath your toes, brambles catching at
your clothes. Hidden hills and gullies that line
the way.
Turning back, you say the journey needs more
time. You are not ready to travel. There is much
to be prepared.
It's an expedition into the unknown, you say,
eyes wide with conviction. A place with a
wildness flowing through it. A great giving up of
attachment to thoughts and things. A giant
giving in to energy in motion and you must be
ready to give your self away.
But my darling girl, while my heart aches to
hear of your travails, this is just a device of your
own making, designed to distract and delay you.
To surrender is not to give up, give in or give
our selves away.
It's a path that has no beginning, end or middle.
The place of surrender is the one that
surrounds us now.
It's the space where we release, and realise that
is what we wish to do.
And it's the space where we listen to the words
of the poem that tells us, she just let go.

My darling girl

I see your struggle to release into the fall.
The fear of heights that stops you standing tall.
The instinct to hold back and reserve some of
your all.
There was a tale for children, of a creature
curled into a ball - it made him feel safe.
And small.
Uncurl, unfurl, my love.
When you step from the high place I will catch
you. When you fall back, my arms will support
you. When you swing wide to the river's far
side, I will hold you.
My darling, I see you stand in a hall of mirrors,
watching your perception of other's perception
of what they perceive you see. In that place you
lose sight of your self and miss the truth of who
is really here. Look up and out and through.
Emerge in your full glory and do not be
ashamed of your light.
Shed your doubt. It serves you no more.
You are held in grace, even as you fall.

My darling girl

You said you couldn't do it.
You said it was too hard. You said you weren't
the type. You said you didn't know how.
You said that it looked scary, that it might hurt,
that you'd be judged.
And then, you took a breath and gripped my
hand... and went and did it anyway.
My gorgeous girl, I couldn't have been prouder!
To take yourself out of your own way, to
tremble and turn that trembling energy into the
power to supercharge your self-belief? That's
well done, my love. That's well done.

My darling girl

You once spoke of a dream. A vision for how things could be. We held hands and talked late into the night, imagining how that dream would feel and taste and look. Exploring all the facets of that vision, we revelled in the picture that you painted. And as you spoke, I saw a single match flare in the darkness, lighting a candle inside you. When the morning came, you laughed at what we'd spoken of, dismissing it as foolish fancy - even while I saw you wished it could be so.

But the candle still burnt true.

Overtime I've seen that flame waver. I've seen that light dim to a glimmer. I've seen you follow others' flames. And I've noticed when you've looked back, to see if your dream was still there, wondering if it's managed to survive, despite all the changes and life stages you have travelled through.

As I look at you today, my love, I see that light is still burning in the night, like the lantern lit for loved ones feared lost at sea.

And though it may have wavered and dimmed at times, I see that dream still calls, and I know if you close your eyes you can see that spark shine still.

If you want to leave it gently burning there, that is your choice, my love.

But remember, if you ever wish to make it burn a little brighter, you just need to give it air. And then you can use it to light your way.

My darling girl

"Be yourself and try to have a good time".
It's a lyric I heard today. And it made me think
of you. It reminded me of that place you
sometimes find yourself in. Tucked in the
shadow. Slightly separate. A little alone. Unsure.
Forgetting who you truly are and how to have a
good time.
But that song was a reminder, my darling.
You can listen to those words, deep in your
heart. You can forget artifice, forget pretence.
Forget not being enough. You can forget being
something other than you are.
And you can simply acknowledge this life isn't
always easy and you can say to yourself, that's
ok. You can soften your heart, your eyes, your
thoughts and release your smile as you feel it
rising. You can play. You can sing. You can
dance. You can hold your head up high. You can
laugh. And, my love, you can allow yourself to
be.

My darling girl

What joy! What joy I see in you today.
This life and love and laughter bubbling through.
Breaking down the crystals of uncertainty,
creating a flow, a rhythm. Embracing this day.
This smooth centred multi-coloured day. A joy
that's vibrant and forgiving. A day made for living.
Sweet and gentle in the spirit, soft and calming in
your soul.

A joy to share, that stretches into a thousand
others' days. A joy that swells with the rising tide
of acknowledged inner affection. A joy that is
shared with no anticipation. A joy that lifts even as
it calms. A joy that brushes your lips with a smile
that holds its fullness deep within your heart.
This joy, is true love.

This is the love you hold for yourself. It's what
confidence is made of. It's what banishes the fears
and helps you see that beyond those fears lies
your heart's desires. It's what gives you strength
and hope and clear sightedness. It's what helps
you love and appreciate others, even if they don't
yet love and appreciate themselves. It's what holds
you and supports you. And it gives me such joy to
see it shining here within you. Making your skin
glow and your eyes shine. Such beauty, my love.
Remember this singing body. Sit inside it. Notice
every tingling aspect of it. Be ready to recall it.

This joy today. It is always there. Even in the
darkest days, its light lives inside you. Ready to be
reached. Ready to shine. It is a part of you. It is a
choice, this joy. And you have chosen wisely.

My darling girl

Run!
Run like the air is free and you have lungs to
breathe it.
Run like the ground is firm and you have feet to
feel it.
Run like your legs are strong, your stride is long.
Run with your arms flung wide, embracing the
air that resists you.
Run with wild abandon.
Run so far, so fast that your laughter trails like a
slipstream behind you.
Run.
And stay centred.
Run.
And feel the calm place within.
Run.
And do not move.
Run.
And listen to every grass blade shift beneath
your feet, flexing down to accept you and then
springing back up as it releases you.
Run.
And see the colours split and dive before your
eyes.
Run.
And feel the world breathe.
Run.
And, my love, be free.

My darling girl

I have you.
I have you held safe in my arms.
I have you despite your hurt and your fear and your feeling that you don't deserve to be loved. I am here, beside you.
My arm around your shoulders, holding you. Not judging you. Ready to move with you into whatever this one life brings.
My sweet heart, this pain you feel. I hold that too. I cradle it in my hands, so you can walk free, unburdened. So you can see it for exactly what it is. So you can look with a clear eye upon it, and name the worries, fears, shame and pain you hold, one by one. And see them. Not as monsters to be feared, but as tiny little parts of you to be loved and cared for. To treat gently, to sooth them so they no longer clamour for endless attention.
I have all of you, held here.
Acknowledging every single aspect of you and loving every single aspect equally.
There's no need to erect barriers, build walls, put up shields, draw a veil. I see you exactly as you are. And I will always love you dearly.
I see your beauty and your strength. I see your wisdom and your truth. I see your compassion and humanity. I see you are enough. And I give you love. Pure, unfettered, deep, abiding, perfect, love.
So be glad, my heart,
and know that you are safe.

My darling girl

Look at all you have achieved.
All the adventures, the challenges,
the grand mistakes, the effortless successes,
the tears and triumphs, the loves,
the friendships, the never-quite-connecteds,
the mountains climbed, rivers swam
and forests you've flown over.
Look at all the things that have brought you to
this place - and remember that all those
resources reside within you.
They are you.
So this fresh future that opens up before you is
one you can enter into with a glad heart and
spring in your step, because you have a pocket
full of everything you need to greet it.
Take heart, dear girl and remember what joy
there is in stepping to the edge of the water and
diving in.
And remember what joy there is in breaking
back through the surface and breathing deeply.
Lungs full and limbs strong. Powerful, present
and perfect in every one of your imperfections.
We are all, all the people we have ever been, and
we hold their lessons with us.
Each one like a flower, ready to be picked when
the time is right.
See that garden you hold within and know it
grows just for you - the life force
to your own growth.
Go. Be. Do.

Henny spent several years working overseas in Spain, Egypt and Portugal, before returning home and finally finding herself in an unexpected corporate career. It was only when she became ill from a combination of grief, stress and poor self-care that she realised she'd lost sight of herself. Her transformative journey to well-being also took her back to learning and post-graduate studies, which informs the work she does today; supporting others through their own change journey.

Henny lives near Cambridge with her husband, son and while there is now just one much-loved dog, it still feels like the house holds two.

Photo credit: Helena g Anderson

GRATITUDE

Every evening I write 21 things I'm grateful for. I know, it might sound a little excessive but it began with a bracelet that had 21 beads, and each thought of gratitude from the day felt like a tiny prayer.

So, here are my 21 beads of gratitude that led to the creation of this little book.

For Soulla without whom the first My darling girl would never have been written, for Lyndsey & Ness my roomies, for all the Soulshiners I've met along the way, for Frances who gave me the mala beads, for Anna and all these sequinned years, for Sophie who shared the very first one, for Belinda Beverley Emma Georgia Hannah Nina Sian & Tracey who all encouraged me to keep sharing, for Carl who chose to publish, for all the WonderWomen & Nottssobad boys & our years that forever bind us, for Emily my oldest friend (though she looks so young!), for the joyful collaboration with Angus, for Abbie who sings of gratitude, for Johnny who'd have loved this, for every friend I haven't named, for my darling family girls, for my darling family boys, for Bibby who loved me, for G who loves me still, for Ru forever, for Anton always, for you reading to the end!

What are you grateful for, dear heart?

Photo credits in order of appearance, all from unsplash.com:

@augustinewong @vork @theamazingdjw @rudonu @creativejunkie
@bekky_bekks @photoart2018 @intuitivmedia @photoart2018
@photoart2018 @bernardhermant @photoart2018 @photoart2018
@wolfgang_hasselmann @shivanshu_oo7 @michaeloeser @gareth_david
@ofisia @timmossholder @denisagati @laurapgevans @beccalavin
@flightarchive @anniespratt @sir_moon @srz @sharonmccutcheon
@sioral8 @anniespratt @ustalo @timmossholder @pavlovyura @sheldonliu
@photoart2018 @anniespratt @autumnstudio @shotz @timmossholder
@my_lens @ofisia @equeen@pawel_czerwinski

Here's something else you might like to know...

We print and distribute from the UK

Our printers only use environmentally certified and recycled papers

All papers are from sustainable sources

We insist on the use of superior quality vegetable based inks

Both we and our printers recycle or reuse all waste products.